Bishop T.D. Jakes, Sr.

Saints with Sinner's Problems

Saints With Sinner's Problems

ISBN 1-890521-02-7

© 1997 T. D. Jakes Enterprises

All rights reserved. Reproduction in whole or part without written permission from the publisher is prohibited. Printed in the United States of America.

All scripture is from the King James Version unless otherwise noted.

T. D. Jakes Enterprises
Dallas, Texas

For years the church has maintained an idealistic concept as it relates to moral issues. We have taught the ideal without admitting the reality! It is not wrong to teach the ideal as long as you acknowledge the reality.

For instance, I hold up a yardstick to a bush that I am hoping will measure thirty-six inches. When I measure it, I find that it is not, in fact, thirty-six inches, but twenty-eight inches. The yardstick becomes the ideal, but the bush is the reality. Now if I lose the yardstick, I will have nothing whereby I can plumb the bush. I then either allow it to become too tall or never stimulate it to reach its fullest potential.

The Word of God becomes the measurement that we are to use to conform our lives into alignment. However, the reality is that most of us have at one time or another fallen miserably short of the ideal.

If we are to continue to grow and recover the distance between our circumstances and His Word, we must teach the ideal and yet treat the reality.

The reality is that there are many people who come to Christ thinking that the moment they become a Christian all of their past ways flee and dissolve. That is not always true. Many people are changed immediately in one area and then struggle for years in another.

Paul writes to the children in the Lord advising them to live free from sin. That is, in fact, the ideal, but He does not leave them struggling with the idea. He also informs them of the "out clause" in case the reality falls short of the ideal.

> *My little children, these things write I unto you, that ye sin not. And if any man sin, we have an advocate with the father, Jesus Christ the righteous and He is the propitiation for our sins: and not for ours only, but also for the sins of the whole world (I John 2:1-2 KJV).*

Going Through Changes

I have known drug addicts who repented of sin and were immediately delivered from their habit with drugs. But even still they were wrestling with cigarettes or jealousy or some other vice. They would say, "I don't see how in the world I can have so much victory in one area and so much defeat in another." Many men become Christians and are committed to the Lord, but at night they wrestle with secret sins like pornography, gambling, or other issues too numerous and some too bizarre to name.

What shall we say to the struggling Christian? What would a shepherd do for a lamb who was caught in a briar? Many Christians are caught in the prickly branches of some unresolved issue!

This is a real struggle to some one who really desires to be right. It can produce guilt and depression; some backslide and leave all together because we, as a church, often do not provide pertinent information that helps them deal with the discomfort of being trapped between two worlds.

Now let's understand some things right now. You must realize that your spirit was created in Christ Jesus when you became a Christian. The spirit or your heart, the very core of your existence is changed immediately! If that has not happened, then salvation is not a reality in your life, and you are just a religious perhaps church-attending, Bible- toting impostor. Your heart, or what we sometimes refer to as your spirit, is immediately changed if authentic salvation has transpired. "And be not conformed to this world: but be ye transformed by the renewing of your mind, that ye may prove what is that good, and acceptable, and perfect will of God." (Romans 12:2 KJV)

What is also true is that your mind is not changed. It is being changed. What is the mind (the soul)? It is the seat, the memories, the will, the desires, the thought patterns, etc., etc. It is being changed by the Word you ingest, digest, and appropriate in your life. That is why you must get the Word of God continually because it helps you to treat the part of you that is under construction! You are saved but not finished. He is still working on those thoughts, memories, tendencies, etc.

"Therefore putting aside all filthiness and all that remains of wickedness, in humility receive the Word implanted, which is able to save your souls" (James 1:21 KJV).

Worse still is the fact that your flesh (body), your appetite, and capacity to perform evil has not been abated. It has not been slain. It must be apprehended. Your body simply is not saved. It will be when Christ returns, but it is not right now.

> *For we know that the whole creation groaneth and travaileth in pain together until now. And not only they, but ourselves also, which have the first fruits of the Spirit, even we ourselves groan within ourselves, waiting for the adoption, to wit, the redemption of our body. For we are saved by hope: but hope that is seen is not hope: for what a man*

seeth, why doth he yet hope for? But if we hope for that we see not, then do we with patience wait for it (Romans 8:22-25 KJV).

No wonder the changed part of you groans trapped inside the unchanged part of you. It is like a clean person trapped in old, filthy clothes. That is uncomfortable. Most of us would not take a shower and manicure ourselves and then dress in old dirty work clothes. It would seem vile.

Yet, God has put a Holy Spirit in a fleshy body that has not been changed into pure holiness. "Why would He do it.?" "It must be uncomfortable," you respond. Of course, it is, but He loves you enough to live in your house until the new one comes!

"Now we know that if the earthly tent we live in is destroyed, we have a building from God, an eternal house in heaven, not built by human hands. Meanwhile we groan, longing to be clothed with our heavenly dwelling, because when we are clothed, we will not be found naked. For while we are in this tent, we groan and are burdened, because we do not wish to be unclothed but to be clothed with our Heavenly dwelling, so that what is mortal may be swallowed up by life. Now it is God who has made us for this very purpose and has given us the Spirit as a *deposit, guaranteeing what is to come*" (2 Cor. 5:15 NIV).

Now let's add this up. My heart is changed, my mind is being changed, and my body is waiting to be changed. If my body is waiting to be changed, what must I do in the meantime to keep from embarrassing my heart by living in such a filthy body?

I am glad you asked the question. It is a sincere but not a new question. Paul asked it also. He says:

> "*For the good that I would I do not: but the evil which I would not, that I do. Now if I do that I would not, it is no more I that do it, but*

sin that dwelleth in me. I find then a law, that, when I would do good, evil is present with me. For I delight in the law of God after the inward man: but I see another law in my members, warring against the law of my mind, and bringing me into captivity to the law of sin which is in my members. O wretched man that I am! Who shall deliver me from the body of this death?" (Romans 7:19-24 KJV)

He later teaches that the body must be dominated until it is recreated. This is discipline. It is not easy, but it is necessary if we are going to be fit for the Master's highest use. We struggle to be used of the Lord when we should struggle to be prepared for the Lord. The body and its tendencies and proclivities have to be enslaved by your desire to please God. If you apprehend it and it breaks the chain, apprehend it again!

All of us have struggled with old issues in one form or another. Teaching your body to obey is the epitome of discipleship. Since it is not saved, it must be enslaved, dominated and controlled. Paul says "but I buffet my body and make it my slave, lest possibly, after I have preached to others, I myself should be disqualified" (Cor. 9:27 NAS).

Get Up! God Is For You.

Probably one of the most difficult parts of the Christian walk is stumbling. If new Christians are taught that in the beginning, they will not become so defeated.

When you were a baby and learning to walk, you did not stand up straight the first day and take off. You will perform fairly similarly in your spiritual walk. You will not be a runner in the beginning. Learn to fall. It's perfectly okay to do so, but what you must remember is that you have to get up and try again. That part of the process is a heyday for Satan. He is watching for you to "mess up" so that he can have a party. His favorite celebration is trapping you into condemnation. Once he weaves you into that web, he will wrap you up tight. You must learn what the Bible says about condemnation and learn to recognize it ever so swiftly. "There is therefore now no condemnation to them which are in Christ Jesus, who walk not after the flesh, but after the Spirit" (Romans 8:1 KJV).

Condemnation is a weapon to hold you at bay while the enemy hurls your past in your face and tells you that you will never make it. God did not start a work in you to abort it because you slipped and tripped. He is not that kind of God. He is ever on your side. He is never watching to see if you fall, but He is always watching to see that you stand. Look at Romans 5:2 and be convinced that there is grace to help you when you are in need. It even says that we stand in grace. Well, new brother or new sister, it seems so incompatible that you could fall and be beaten while you are standing.

Learn to believe what God says about you. He is a loving Father. He is on your side, cheering you every step of the way. The Holy Ghost is referred to as a helper, also as a coach. God is out there on the sidelines saying, "Come on, get up you can make it. I am with you." He will never leave you or forsake you.

Right now if you have an image, an old erroneous idea of who God is, one that depicts Him as a harsh taskmaster, get rid of that at this moment. He will be for you when everyone is against you, with you when you are all alone, cheering for you when others are jeering at you, and loving you when you don't even love yourself. Now that's some kind of Father!!

Any issue that a new Christian might confront is a good topic for discussion. Where did anyone start the rumor that after you become a Christian, you become a rose and the world gets rosy? Not so. Often times, these are very difficult times for a Christian.

The enemy is upset because he lost his grip on you, and wants to really work on your mind so that you would never think about witnessing. That is one of his oldest tricks. If you even look like you might be telling someone about Jesus, the devil will make you feel like every vice you ever had is written on your forehead for everybody to see. Be certain of this, too: When you do mess up, he loves to give you an audience. He realizes where you are weak, so he does have some ammunition to play with, but your armor is stronger than his accusations.

Go on and share the love of Jesus. That way your testimony will be validated unquestionably by the personal grace evident in your life. That person will be introduced to the love of the Father who welcomes home dirty, backslidden, prodigal children. Isn't He wonderful?

This world is still under a god. Yes, that's right. The Bible refers to the devil as the "god of this world," and the "prince of the power of the air." He's still here. All of the crime, hate, violence, and heartache will still be here after you get saved. The world will not be saved, but you will be. Jesus says that "you are in the world, but you are not of the world." Now that leaves you with some choices. The world dictates a tremendous amount of power over how people think, what they wear, how they act, how they react, what is politically correct, what entertainment we are subjected to, and a host of other areas where the influence is strong.

The Bible tells us to "come out from among them." What that means is to separate yourself from situations and environments that will place you in a compromising position.

If you had a drinking problem, get rid of everything including the cough syrup that has a high alcoholic content. Flee from those places where you used to hang out. The place is still there, those people are still there, but you must stay away. If cigarettes are a problem, get someone to pray with you for deliverance and make sure you stay away from people who smoke and places where smoking is commonplace. You will have to change the circuit you once traveled. If not, you will be setting yourself up for the same old problems that had you bound before. Each day you need to ask God to direct your steps, but you are wearing the shoes. I can remember the old timers saying, "Don't go anywhere you wouldn't want to be found when Jesus returns for you."

Ladies especially will have some real decisions to make concerning attire. The way the world has molded and shaped the fashion industry is not at all reflective of the image a Christian woman of God wants to exude. The dress of a Christian woman can be beautiful and stylish. There is no suggestion that God wants women to be bound up by legalistic restrictions on what they can and cannot wear. The usage God wants portrayed is beauty with His mark of approval on it. Short skirts and low-cut blouses are suggestive. That is totally inappropriate for a lady who represents God. Women, you can be beautiful, but emphasize what God is doing in your heart by what you wear for the world to see.

> *Do not let your adornment be merely outward-arranging the hair, wearing gold, or putting on fine apparel-rather let it be the hidden person of the heart, with the incorruptible beauty of a gentle and quiet spirit, which is very precious in the sight of God. For in this manner, in former times the holy women who trusted in God also adorned themselves, being submissive to their own husbands (I Peter*

3:3-6 NKJV).

How To Live Holy

You will be surrounded by temptations everywhere you go. The world is a very seductive place to live. It is difficult to find friends who want to be sold out to God. Avoid those people who want to remain in the old lifestyle. You may have to shake off a few, but in the long run God will replace them with people with whom you can be "equally yoked." You will want to remain close to people who are hungry for God and who remember the past only long enough to say, "I do not want to go back there."

The Bible tells us that God has a future for us that is good. Keep seeking God and

He will take you to the promised land. Why would you want to risk exposing yourself to the old temptations? If you were promiscuous, stay far from those people with whom you sinned. The Bible says:

> "Know ye not that your bodies are the members of Christ? Shall I then take the members of Christ and make them the members of an harlot? God forbid. What? Know ye not that He which is joined to a harlot is one body? For TWO, saith he, SHALL BE ONE FLESH. But he that is joined unto the Lord is one spirit."

> "Flee fornication. Every sin

that a man doeth is without the body; but He that committeth fornication sinneth against his own body. What? Know ye not that your body is the temple of the Holy Ghost which is in you, which ye have of God, and ye are not your own?" (I Cor. 6: 15-19 KJV)

The Word says to "flee." That means to stay as far away from it as you can get. Never place yourself in a situation where you may have to compromise. Just spare yourself from having to make a choice. Avoid the situation completely. Don't ever think that you will be able to resist the temptation. The Bible says God will provide a way of escape, but that could mean the way is the opposite direction of where the problem will be awaiting you. If you do not return to your old hang-outs, you will avoid the temptations. Eventually, you will have severed every desire to return because all your fulfillment will come from God.

Another problem you will confront is that of your old "buddies." If they are not going to come to church with you, be careful that you do not go to clubs with them.

Set up some new standards of where you will and will not go. You are in a very vulnerable stage of your walk as a new convert. Avoid those people who would like to take you back to where you were and where they are. Make some acquaintances with like-minded believers, people who want all God has. You may just have to say good-bye permanently to those who would love to see you in the same hell that they have chosen to stay in. FLEE. You have made up your mind to follow Jesus. Yes, the problems will all still be there, but you now have a powerful new FRIEND who can take you through any situation that the world, the devil, or you, yourself will bring your way.

In closing, do not be discouraged. Keep on keeping on. The journey begins with a single step. If you do mess up, and we all do, God is gracious and Jesus is ever interceding on your behalf. He wants you to come out on top. The past is over, yet it will try to creep back into your thought life. Protect your mind with the Word of God. Let the Bible be your companion. Learn to be who God says you are, and you will find that victory is yours in Jesus!! "These things have I spoken unto you, that in me ye might have peace. In the world ye shall have tribulation: but be of good cheer; I have overcome the world." (John 16:33 KJV) AND SO CAN YOU!

About The Author

Bishop T. D. Jakes was born and raised in Charleston, West Virginia. He has been ministering the gospel of Jesus Christ for twenty years. He established and continued his pastorate as founder and Senior Pastor of Temple of Faith Ministries in Charleston, West Virginia for sixteen years. In July, 1996, Bishop Jakes relocated, along with T. D. Jakes Ministries, to Dallas, Texas. He serves as Senior Pastor of one of the fastest growing mega churches in the country. The Potter's House is a church home base at which T. D. Jakes' national ministry resides.

Bishop Jakes is a vibrant and charismatic minister. Although he holds an earned Doctorate of Ministry to his credit, his ministry is noted for deep inner healing and practical application of Christian principles to the tragedies of life. Furthermore, he is a highly celebrated and accomplished author of six bestsellers: *Woman, Thou Art Loosed*, *Naked And Not Ashamed*, *Can You Stand To Be Blessed?*, *Daddy Loves His Girls*, *The Harvest*, and *Loose The Man And Let Him Go*, along with several other books that have become quite popular. He also serves on the board of directors and as a contributing writer for several religious magazines.

Bishop Jakes is reaching the nation through his weekly television broadcast, "Get Ready with T.D. Jakes," which airs three times a week on Trinity Broadcasting Network (TBN) and Black Entertainment Television (BET). His broadcast has reached international proportion, being aired throughout the Caribbean, South Africa, Zimbabwe and several other countries around the world!

Bishop Jakes is the CEO for T. D. Jakes Ministries which has successfully promoted hundreds of conferences across the country. Its "Woman, Thou Art Loosed", "Manpower" and annual Bible Conferences average from 5,000 to 20,000 people in attendance.

Bishop Jakes is obviously a very involved minister, but aside from these many ministerial duties, he is the husband to his lovely wife, Serita. They are the proud parents of five wonderful children. We are proud to present him to you. This is a man on a mission. He is uniquely articulate and highly respected. His ministry is setting a precedence of excellence.

Bishop T.D. Jakes

Also By T.D. Jakes

SINGLE CASSETTES/VIDEOS

I Am Still In His Hands	☐ $6 ☐ $20
The Kingdom Is Going To The Dogs	☐ $6 ☐ $20
Your Faith Must Stand Trial	☐ $6 ☐ $20
The Struggle Is Over	☐ $6 ☐ $20
When The Dove Cries	☐ $6 ☐ $20
Remember Lot's Wife	☐ $6 ☐ $20
The Spell Is Broken	☐ $6 ☐ $20
The Power of The Cross	☐ $6 ☐ $20
Pass The Bread	☐ $6 ☐ $20
Get Away From The Gate	☐ $6 ☐ $20
If You Can Give It Up, You Can Have It All	☐ $6 ☐ $20
Now!	☐ $6 ☐ $20
Provoked	☐ $6 ☐ $20
He Called Me Son	☐ $6 ☐ $20
After This I Want My Stuff	☐ $6 ☐ $20
The Blessed Man	☐ $6 ☐ $20
Loose That Man And Let Him Go	☐ $6 ☐ $20
The Price Of Power	☐ $6 ☐ $20
Overcoming Silent Frustrations	☐ $6 ☐ $20
Questions From The Cross	☐ $6 ☐ $20
Chosen	☐ $6 ☐ $20
The King Has A Crippled Child	☐ $6 ☐ $20
Breaking The Spirit Of Failure	☐ $6 ☐ $20
Leftovers	☐ $6 ☐ $20
Naked And Not Ashamed	☐ $6 ☐ $20
The Light Of The Word	☐ $6 ☐ $20
Here Comes My Old Friend Again	☐ $6 ☐ $20
Seeing What You Believe	☐ $6 ☐ $20
This Is Not My Will To Be Like This	☐ $6 ☐ $20
Rags To Riches	☐ $6 ☐ $20

BOOKS/WORKBOOKS

Woman Thou Art Loosed	$9.95
Woman Thou Art Loosed/Wkbk.	$6.95
Can You Stand To Be Blessed?	$9.95
Can You Stand.../Wkbk.	$6.95
Water In The Wilderness	$6.95
Why?	$8.95
Why?/Notebook	$6.95
Naked And Not Ashamed	$11.95
Help, I've Fallen And Can't Get Up	$6.95
A Fresh Glimpse Of The Dove/Study Guide	$11.00
When Shepherds Bleed/Wkbk.	$10.00
Loose That Man And Let Him Go	$11.95
Loose That Man.../Wkbk.	$6.95
Harvest	$8.95
Harvest/Workbook	$6.95
Daddy Loves His Girls	$11.95

MINI-BOOKS

Lord, I Said I Wouldn't Fail You, But I Did!
Lord, I Miss My Time With You
Have You Received Since You Believed?
But, I Can't Afford To Tithe
Tithing Is A Matter Of Love...Not Law
Provoke God With Your Giving
I Choose To Forgive!
Saints With Sinner's Problems
Water Baptism: Who Needs It?
Help Me To Fit In My Own Church
Winning The Battle In Your Own Mind
It's Not Natural To Live Holy, It's Spiritual

A complete list of conferences, tapes, videos and books by
T.D. Jakes is available by writing:
T.D. Jakes • P.O. Box 5390 • Dallas, TX 75208